L WAR ★

RECONSTRUCTION

Rebuilding America after the Civil War

By Stephanie Fitzgerald

Content Adviser: Brett Barker, PhD,
Assistant Professor of History,
University of Wisconsin–Marathon County

Reading Adviser: Alexa L. Sandmann, EdD, Professor of Literacy,
College and Graduate School of Education, Health, and
Human Services, Kent State University

COMPASS POINT BOOKS
a capstone imprint

Compass Point Books
151 Good Counsel Drive
P.O. Box 669
Mankato, MN 56002-0669

Printed in the United States of America in Stevens Point, Wisconsin.
032010
005741WZF10

 This book was manufactured with paper containing
at least 10 percent post-consumer waste.

Managing Editor: Catherine Neitge
Designer: Heidi Thompson
Media Researcher: Svetlana Zhurkin
Library Consultant: Kathleen Baxter
Production Specialist: Jane Klenk
Cartographer: XNR Productions, Inc.

Library of Congress Cataloging-in-Publication Data
Fitzgerald, Stephanie.
  Reconstruction: rebuilding America after the Civil War / by Stephanie Fitzgerald.
      p. cm.—(The Civil War)
  Includes bibliographical references and index.
  ISBN 978-0-7565-4370-9 (library binding)
  ISBN 978-0-7565-4414-0 (paperback)
1. Reconstruction (U.S. history, 1865–1877)—Juvenile literature.
2. United States—History—1865–1898—Juvenile literature. I. Title. II. Series.
  E668.B945 2011
  973.8—dc22   2010001019

Image Credits: Getty Images: Hulton Archive, 27, Time & Life Pictures/Mansell, 18;
Library of Congress, 3 (left and right), 5, 6, 8, 10, 12, 15, 22, 25, 33, 37, 41, 43, 45, 46,
48, 51, 53, 55, 56 (right), 57 (all); North Wind Picture Archives, cover, 3 (middle), 17,
28, 35, 56 (left).

Visit Compass Point Books on the Internet at *www.capstonepub.com*

TABLE OF
CONTENTS

CHAPTER 1
A DIVIDED NATION

On April 11, 1865, President Abraham Lincoln appeared before a crowd of excited—and expectant—citizens in Washington, D.C. Just two days earlier, Confederate General Robert E. Lee had surrendered to Union General Ulysses S. Grant at Appomattox Court House, Virginia. The long, bloody Civil War was finally over.

Many people thought Lincoln would give a victory speech. Although his speech celebrated the Union triumph, it was more somber than many might have expected. The president warned that there was still much work to do to restore the nation. He said, in part:

"We meet this evening, not in sorrow, but in gladness of heart. [The] surrender of the principal insurgent army, [gives] hope of a righteous and speedy peace whose joyous expression can not be restrained. …

"By these recent successes the re-inauguration of the national authority—reconstruction—which has had a large share of thought from the first, is pressed much more closely upon our attention. It is fraught with great difficulty."

When Lincoln spoke about reconstruction, he was talking about the process of bringing the nation back together. The war had accomplished the goal of keeping the United States together as one country. The Confederate states, which had broken away from the Union and formed their own country, had been defeated. Because the South had lost the war, there was no longer a country called the Confederate States of America. But the United States now faced the task of rebuilding the war-torn South—and re-establishing good relations among all citizens.

Just as important, the Civil War had put an end to slavery. It was up to the federal government, and all Americans, to help 4 million former slaves begin a life of freedom. What

Abraham Lincoln delivered his 1865 inaugural address on the east portico of the U.S. Capitol.

would follow slavery in the South, and what would life be like for black Americans? Reconstruction, as the president said, was not going to be easy.

★HUNDREDS OF THOUSANDS LOST

The Civil War began in 1861 soon after 11 southern states formed the Confederate States of America. Both sides—the Union and the Confederacy—expected a quick victory. Instead the fighting dragged on for four years. By the time it finally ended, the war had claimed the lives of more than 620,000 American soldiers—360,000 Yankees and at least 260,000 rebels.

The devastation was particularly widespread in the South,

Soldiers' graves in City Point, Virginia

where much of the fighting took place. The plantations and farms that had provided food and income for southerners, rich and poor, had been damaged or destroyed. Farm animals had been slaughtered. Entire cities had been reduced to piles of rubble. People all over the South—including newly freed slaves—were homeless. Thousands starved to death.

THE EMANCIPATION PROCLAMATION

At the start of the Civil War, President Lincoln made it clear that the only northern war goal was to preserve the Union. He, like most northerners, did not support ending slavery. As the war raged on, however, slaves began to seize freedom for themselves. Black men, women, and children began leaving plantations and heading for Union Army camps. In January 1863 Lincoln issued the Emancipation Proclamation.

It read, in part, that "all persons held as slaves within any State or designated part of a State, the people whereof shall then be in rebellion against the United States, shall be then, thenceforward, and forever free." The proclamation did not immediately free many slaves. It only referred to slaves in Confederate states— most of which were not under Union control—and so a Union victory was needed for it to be effective. But it did announce a new aim of the war: the destruction of slavery in the United States.

Richmond, Virginia, was in ruins at the end of the Civil War.

The South was absolutely destitute. Many structures—such as buildings, bridges, and railroad tracks—were in ruins, and there was no money to rebuild. The morale of southerners who had supported the Confederacy also suffered a serious blow. They were bitter in defeat and, in many ways, refused to accept that they had been conquered. Many found it nearly impossible to believe they had lost the war. They could hardly comprehend the idea that their slaves were now free. There was no way they would even consider that black people ever would—or could—be equal to whites.

★HEALING OLD WOUNDS

From the start of the war, President Lincoln had been planning for the reunification of the country. He wanted to heal the wounds as quickly as possible, even while the war went on. In December 1863, Lincoln proposed what became known as the Ten Percent Plan. Under the plan, southern men who swore loyalty to the United States and recognized the freedom of former slaves would be granted amnesty for their acts of rebellion. High-ranking officials of the Confederate government and military were temporarily excluded. After one-tenth of the white male voters in a state had taken the oath, that state would be allowed to create a new government and elect representatives to the U.S. Congress. Under the plan, states that had seceded could be readmitted to the Union.

Some Republicans in Congress, who became known as Radical Republicans, disliked Lincoln's Reconstruction plan. They felt it was too lenient. In February 1864 Senator Benjamin F. Wade of Ohio and Representative Henry Winter Davis of Maryland proposed a stricter plan. Their proposal, called the Wade-Davis bill, would have required that a majority of each state's men take a loyalty oath. The bill also would have made it nearly impossible for former Confederate officials to take part in the political process. (They could neither have voted nor held office.) The bill passed in Congress, but it was vetoed by President Lincoln in July. He was determined to make it as easy as possible for the former rebel states to rejoin the Union.

Meanwhile, the question of what would happen to newly freed slaves remained to be answered. By 1865 tens of thousands of slaves had run away from their owners and reached safety behind Union lines or with Union armies. The freedmen, as they were called, had little or no property, and most could neither read nor write. Union generals wrote to their superiors in Washington requesting guidance on how to deal with the freedmen. The federal government responded

Former Virginia slaves faced an uncertain future in 1865.

FORTY ACRES AND A MULE

During the war thousands of black refugees had followed General William T. Sherman's army. In January 1865 Sherman and Secretary of War Edwin M. Stanton met with leaders of the black community in Savannah, Georgia, to discuss the future of former slaves.

Garrison Frazier, a former slave who had bought his freedom eight years earlier, spoke for the group: "The way we can best take care of ourselves is to have land, and turn it and till it by our own labor—that is, by the labor of the women and children and old men; and we can soon maintain ourselves and have something to spare. … We want to be placed on land until we are able to buy it and make it our own."

Four days later Sherman issued Special Field Orders, No. 15. The order called for seizing about 400,000 acres (162,000 hectares) of land stretching from South Carolina to Florida and turning it over to newly freed black families. Each family would receive a 40-acre (16-hectare) plot. Anyone who needed a mule could borrow one from the Army. The order also said that "exclusive management of affairs will be left to the freed people themselves, subject only to the United States military authority, and the acts of Congress." The plan seemed like fitting compensation for the former slaves. But the arrangement did not last.

by creating the Bureau of Refugees, Freedmen and Abandoned Lands—known as the Freedmen's Bureau—in March 1865.

Offices of the Freedmen's Bureau were set up all across the South. Agents distributed food, medicine, and clothing to people in need—both black and white. They also set up schools for former slaves, and helped them make the transition to freedom.

Lincoln was assassinated while attending a play in Washington, D.C.

The first difficult steps toward Reconstruction had been taken, but the country still did not have a solid plan. Who would prevail— Radical Republicans in Congress or President Lincoln? On April 14 that question became moot when Lincoln was fatally shot. The country looked to his successor, Andrew Johnson, to set the tone. Former slaves, however, were not waiting for a government plan. They immediately set about building new lives.

CHAPTER 2
FOREVER FREE

After emancipation African-Americans in the South
quickly tried to take control of their destinies. They knew
education and land ownership were crucial to success.
Just as important was the ability to worship freely and to
re-establish their families.

Many freed people realized that education was the first step
toward improving their position in life. "What would the best
soil produce without cultivation?" asked a former slave. "We
want to get wisdom. That is all we need. Let us get that, and we
are made for time and eternity."

Before the Civil War, most southern states had made it
illegal to teach a slave to read or write. In addition, slaves
were punished—with whippings or beatings—if they tried
to teach themselves. Any slave who managed to learn these
skills kept his or her knowledge a carefully guarded secret.

During the war Union Army officers, northern
missionaries, abolitionists, and representatives of freedmen's
organizations traveled to Union-controlled southern states to

DAVID WALKER'S APPEAL

An anti-slavery document that appeared in 1829 caused widespread panic in the South. It was *David Walker's Appeal to the Coloured Citizens of the World.* The author, David Walker, was born in North Carolina to a slave father and a free mother. Because his mother was free, Walker also was free. Nevertheless, he witnessed the evils of slavery firsthand—including a young slave's being forced to whip his mother to death. In *David Walker's Appeal*, the author encouraged slaves to rise against their oppressors. He wrote, in part: "It is no more harm for you to kill a man, who is trying to kill you, than it is for you to take a drink of water when thirsty." The publication led many southern states to forbid the education of blacks. It even led to death threats. Indeed, Walker died in 1830 under mysterious circumstances.

set up schools for newly freed people. Former slaves who could read and write also began holding classes. There were classes wherever space could be found—in churches, abandoned buildings, and even former slave markets.

Many teachers who came south were black. As more former slaves were educated, they too became teachers. Many of today's well known historically black colleges were established during this time. Howard University was founded in Washington, D.C., in 1867. It was named for

Major General Oliver O. Howard, a commissioner of the Freedmen's Bureau and one of the school's founders. A year earlier, the school that would become Fisk University was founded in Tennessee. In 1868 Hampton Institute was chartered in Virginia. By 1869 there were more black teachers than white teaching freed people in the South.

Many white southerners believed it was dangerous to teach black people to read and write. They worried that it would make former slaves think they were equal to whites. Many used violence to try to stop people from educating

Students studied physics at Hampton Institute.

former slaves. They burned down schools and threatened teachers—even attacking many. A story in the *New Orleans Tribune* described violence against schoolteachers. It read, in part: "They have whipped Mr. LeBlanc at Point Coupee; dangerously stabbed in the back Mr. Burnham at Monroe; and beaten almost to death Mr. Ruby at Jackson. The record of the teachers of the first colored schools in Louisiana will be one of honor and blood."

★FREE TO WORSHIP

Some white southerners also felt threatened by the black churches that were beginning to spring up. When they were enslaved, African-Americans were forced to worship as their owners did. They attended white churches, where they sat in the back of the building or in galleries on the second floor. Slaves often held their own secret services on plantations. After the war black people formed their own churches and selected their own preachers.

Soon the church became the most important institution in black communities. Besides being places of worship, they were used as schools and places to hold political meetings. Ministers, often the best educated black people in the communities, had great influence over their congregations. They used their pulpits to encourage church members to fight for equal rights.

African-Americans spent many hours at church each week for services and community activities.

For African-Americans, a big part of being free meant reuniting families that had been broken apart by slavery, as well as creating legal unions between spouses. Marriages between slaves did not have legal standing, even though slaves considered their marriages real. After emancipation tens of thousands of newly freed people registered their marriages with the Army, local governments, and the Freedmen's Bureau. Many tried to find family members they had been separated from during slavery.

Slave owners did not seem to worry about separating

Newly freed slaves were finally allowed to legally wed.

families when they wanted to sell some of their workers. More often than not, wives, husbands, and their children were sold to different plantation owners. Frequently slaves were sold across state lines. They might also be sold more than once in a lifetime. It was safe to assume that a slave who was sold away would never see his or her family again. After emancipation thousands of freed people tried desperately to find their loved ones. All too often, they were unsuccessful.

CIVIL RIGHTS ADVOCATE

Thaddeus Stevens, a leader of the House Radical Republicans, was born into a poor family in 1792. Despite his obvious intelligence, poverty and physical deformity made Stevens an outcast for much of his early life. For the rest of his days, Stevens used his power to promote a truly equal American society. As an attorney, he frequently defended runaway and fugitive slaves. He was very active in the Underground Railroad and eventually made the abolition of slavery his primary goal. While serving in Congress, Stevens was one of the most outspoken advocates for African-American rights before and during Reconstruction.

When he died in 1868, about 20,000 people attended his funeral in his hometown of Lancaster, Pennsylvania. Stevens chose to be buried in Schreiner-Concord Cemetery because it was the only one in Lancaster that accepted people of all races. The inscription he wrote for his headstone reads: "I repose in this quiet and secluded spot, not from any natural preference for solitude, but finding other cemeteries limited as to race, by charter rules, I have chosen this that I might illustrate in my death the principles which I advocated through a long life, equality of man before his Creator."

★A CHANCE AT INDEPENDENCE

More than almost anything else, freed people wanted to have their own land. They thought owning property would truly free them from the influence of whites. They could support their families with their own crops and work for themselves—without the supervision of white overseers. They also believed that years of harsh, unpaid labor had earned them the right to these lands. Immediately after the war, it seemed as though this dream would come true.

In June 1865, five months after General William T. Sherman issued his Special Field Orders, No. 15, which gave land to former slaves, more than 10,000 freed people were farming almost 500,000 acres (202,343 hectares) of land. Representative Thaddeus Stevens of Pennsylvania and other abolitionists proposed expanding Sherman's plan. They wanted the government to seize the land of rich former Confederates and divide it among freed people. "We propose to confiscate all the estate of every rebel belligerent whose estate was worth $10,000 or whose land exceeded two hundred acres in quantity," Stevens said. "Give if you please forty acres to each adult male freedman." Before that could happen, however, Congress and the new president, Andrew Johnson, had to hammer out a workable plan for Reconstruction.

CHAPTER 3
THE FIGHT TO REBUILD THE NATION

As former slaves pursued a life of freedom, Congress and President Johnson worked on a plan for Reconstruction. Many felt that Lincoln's plan was too easy on the rebelling states. They hoped his successor, a Democrat from Tennessee, would create a harsher plan. Johnson had been the only southern senator who remained in Congress—and stayed loyal to the Union—when his state seceded. Now the country would see where he truly stood on the issues. Many would be disappointed.

Johnson had opposed secession, but he was by no means an abolitionist. The new president had owned five slaves before the war and was prejudiced against black people. Johnson hated the rich plantation owners of the South—the so-called planter aristocracy. Although he would try to punish the richest rebels, he had no interest in helping newly freed slaves. "This is a country for white men," he said, "and by God, as long as I am President, it shall be a government for white men."

He also wanted to avoid punishing southerners who did not have slaves.

Johnson was a former tailor who learned how to read and write as a teenager. Through hard work, he rose from poverty to the highest office in the land. The new president identified with the small farmers and craftsmen who made up most of the South's white population. It was not surprising that he disliked rich planters.

On May 29, 1865, Johnson set forth his plan for amnesty. Most Confederates would be pardoned and would get their property back—except for their slaves. All these men had to do was take an oath of allegiance to the United States and support the emancipation of slaves.

It appeared that the president would not be nearly as generous with those who had held high-ranking positions in the Confederate government or military. "Traitors must be impoverished," he said. "They must not only be punished, but their social power must

Andrew Johnson was military governor of Tennessee before serving as Lincoln's vice president.

be destroyed." Johnson soon relented, however. Everyone who had been excluded from the general amnesty had the option of applying to Johnson in person for a pardon. Nearly everyone who applied received the president's pardon.

By the end of 1865, Johnson had pardoned 13,000 people whom he had previously labeled traitors. Many of the former Confederates were then elected to new state governments in the South. Alexander Stephens, the former vice president of the Confederacy, was even elected to the U.S. Congress.

None of the new state government officials elected in the South were black. Benjamin Franklin Perry, the provisional governor of South Carolina, summed up the popular attitude. "This is a white man's government, intended for white men only," he said. It did not take long for the southern governments to limit the newly won freedoms of black people.

★AN UNFAIR SHARE

When all the pardoned rebels' confiscated land was returned, the promise of 40 acres died. Many freed people fought to keep the land they had claimed, but it was a losing proposition. Union troops had to forcibly remove some people from the land. A bitter reality soon became clear: Many black people would be forced to work once again for whites.

Agents of the Freedmen's Bureau worked with black workers and white employers to create fair labor contracts.

THE 13TH AMENDMENT

The 13th Amendment to the Constitution, which formally abolished slavery throughout the United States, was ratified December 6, 1865. The amendment provides: "Neither slavery nor involuntary servitude, except as a punishment for crime whereof the party shall have been duly convicted, shall exist within the United States, or any place subject to their jurisdiction." Former Confederate states were expected, but not required, to ratify the amendment in order to rejoin the Union. All of the states ratified the amendment, although it took until the 20th century for three to do so: Delaware in 1901, Kentucky in 1976, and Mississippi in 1995.

Despite the agents' efforts, however, both parties were often dissatisfied. Black people usually found that paid work did not differ greatly from slave work. Most of the time they lived in former slave quarters, worked many hours every day in the fields, and still were under the watchful eyes of white overseers. Planters resented the interference of the Freedmen's Bureau agents—but not as much as they resented not being allowed to use physical punishment to "encourage" their employees to work hard.

In areas where cotton and tobacco were grown,

sharecropping became a common form of wage labor. A planter would provide a freedman with a piece of land, a place to live, and everything he would need to grow crops: seeds, livestock, and farm machinery. The sharecropper would plant and harvest the crops and then give them to the planter. In most cases, the planter would sell the crops and give the sharecropper a percentage—a share—after deducting for expenses. Sometimes the planter would give the sharecropper part of the crops to sell on his own.

Many freed people preferred sharecropping to ordinary labor because it let them work for themselves, to some

Men, women, and children picked cotton in Georgia after the war.

extent. They hoped they would be able to save enough of their profits to buy their own land some day. The sharecropping system, however, was set up to prevent that from happening.

Most sharecroppers were not paid until their crops were harvested, so they did not have much cash. They were forced to buy necessities, such as food and clothing, on credit. They often bought them from the landholder, who charged outrageous prices. After a sharecropper paid off his expenses from his share of a crop, he had little or no money left.

★A NEW FORM OF CONTROL

With slavery outlawed, white southerners looked for legal ways to re-create the conditions black people had been subject to under slavery. In the summer of 1865, southern legislatures passed laws, called Black Codes, to further limit the rights of freed people.

The first Black Codes were passed in Mississippi, and then the idea spread throughout the South. South Carolina had one of the harshest codes. Under its laws, freed people could work only as field hands or servants unless they obtained a special license and paid a fee. Servants were expected to work all day—from sunrise to sunset—and their employers were allowed to whip them "moderately." Former slaves who signed a contract to work on a plantation were not allowed to leave the property without permission of their employer.

Under many Black Codes, freedmen could not own guns, nor could they gather in large groups. Such rules had been in effect during the years of slavery to prevent uprisings. After the war many white southerners feared that former slaves would exact bloody revenge for their years of abuse. The new restrictions on recently freed people would keep them from organizing and retaliating against their former

Black workers used horse-drawn plows to plant sugarcane in the late 1860s.

owners. The new laws—like all Black Codes—were meant to keep freedmen on unequal footing with whites.

The Black Codes said children who were orphaned, or whose parents had no job or permanent home, could be forced to work for white employers. Courts could, and did, apprentice the children to employers against their will. If they tried to run away, they could be physically punished.

There were also separate laws—and court systems—

Former slaves were severely punished even after obtaining their freedom.

for blacks and whites. Any freed person who did not have a job could be charged with vagrancy and forced to work for a white person for up to a year. Black people who were found guilty of minor crimes could be whipped or made to work for white people. These penalties were never imposed on white lawbreakers. Certain crimes carried the death penalty for black people, but not for whites. These included crimes that whites thought freedmen were likely to commit, including rebellion, burglary, and assaulting white women.

★ A RADICAL RESPONSE

When people in the North heard about the Black Codes, many of them were outraged. The laws, a southerner admitted, were an attempt "to restore all of slavery but its name." Many northerners strongly felt that former slaves should be free to live without interference from whites. Some thought the codes made a mockery of the Union victory in the Civil War. "We tell the white men of Mississippi," thundered the *Chicago Tribune*, "that the men of the North will convert the state of Mississippi into a frog-pond before they will allow any such laws to disgrace one foot of soil over which the flag of freedom waves."

The Radical Republicans in Congress were already angry about President Johnson's Reconstruction plan.

The Black Codes increased their desire to create their own plan. First Congress refused to allow representatives and senators from southern states to take their seats. Johnson claimed that Reconstruction was substantially complete, and he demanded that the southern delegates be accepted. In response, Congress investigated conditions in the South under Johnson's Reconstruction plan and labeled the plan a failure. In December 1865 Thaddeus Stevens argued that Congress could not ignore the plight of former slaves:

"We have turned, or are about to turn, loose four million slaves without a hut to shelter them or a cent in their pockets. The infernal laws of slavery have prevented them from acquiring an education, understanding the common laws of contract, or of managing the ordinary business of life. This Congress is bound to provide for them until they can take care of themselves. If we do not furnish them with homesteads, and hedge them around with protective laws; if we leave them to the legislation of their late masters, we had better have left them in bondage. If we fail in this great duty now, when we have the power, we shall deserve and receive the [condemnation] of history and of all future ages."

Two months later Congress passed a bill to extend the life of the Freedmen's Bureau. It was also intended to give the bureau more power to protect former slaves from the Black Codes. President Johnson vetoed the bill, claiming that it was up to the states to determine what the laws within their borders would be. The Senate majority's vote total was one short of the number needed to override Johnson's veto, and the bill died.

In March Congress passed the Civil Rights Act of 1866. The bill would grant citizenship, and guarantee the rights enjoyed by white people, to all men, "without distinction of race or color, or previous condition of slavery or involuntary servitude." This would ensure that the inequality of laws such as the Black Codes—one set of penalties for black people, another for whites—would no longer be allowed.

As before, Johnson vetoed the Civil Rights Act. He made

many complaints about it, including a claim that "the distinction of race and color is by the bill made to operate in favor of the colored against the white race." This time, however, Congress had enough votes to override the president's veto. The bill became law in April.

Johnson's veto of the Civil Rights Act cost him support in Congress. The Radical Republicans saw a chance to remake Reconstruction, and they decided to seize it. The party's goal was summed up by Thaddeus Stevens: "Every man, no matter what his race or color, every earthly being who has an immortal soul, has an equal right to justice, honesty and fair play with every other man; and the law should secure him those rights."

Congress voted to approve the 14th Amendment to the U.S. Constitution in June 1866. The amendment declares that "All persons born or naturalized in the United States and subject to the jurisdiction thereof, are citizens of the United States and of the State wherein they reside." By including black people in this group of citizens, the amendment ensured that their civil rights would be protected by the government. The amendment also disqualified anyone who had "engaged in insurrection or rebellion" against the United States from holding federal or state office. The 14th Amendment did not require southern states to allow black men to vote. But it did provide that any state that did not do so would lose some

MENDING THE FAMILY KETTLE.

An 1866 political cartoon criticizes President Johnson for taking too long to help the South. The caption has Columbia saying: "Now, Andy, I wish you and your boys would hurry up that job, because I want to use that kettle right away. You are all talking too much about it."

representation in Congress and some electoral votes in presidential elections.

Johnson attacked the amendment, which widened the divide between Congress and the president. His reaction also encouraged the former Confederate states (except Tennessee) to reject the amendment, which they did.

★A BLOODY REACTION

As Congress and the president debated, black people across the South were being violently attacked. After the former rebels were pardoned for their part in the Civil War, they lost all fear of the federal government—if they'd had any to begin with. As the government worked to stop the legal discrimination and abuse of freed people, many whites turned to terrorist tactics.

Black people were threatened, beaten, and even killed with alarming frequency. There was no punishment. In Tennessee a white farmer, Amos Black, told one of his freed workers to return a pair of oxen to their owner. The worker, Tom, didn't know the way. He suggested that his brother go instead. Black's response was to shoot Tom in the head. "You have been fooled with the damned Yankee lies till you thought you were free, and you got so you could not obey your master," Black announced to the other workers. "There is no law against killing niggers and I will kill every damned one I have, if they do not obey me and work just as hard as they did before the war."

Black's attitude was typical of many whites in the South. In 1865 a white supremacy group, the Ku Klux Klan, was founded by a group of former Confederate soldiers. Its aim was to create an atmosphere of violence and intimidation that would prevent black people from using the rights they had gained. The Klan hoped to force blacks—and whites—

to renounce the Republican Party and the whole idea of Reconstruction.

Full-scale riots broke out across the South. The worst race riot in the history of Memphis, Tennessee, raged from April 30 to May 2, 1866. Forty-six African-Americans and two white people were killed. Ninety-one homes burned, and eight schools and four churches were destroyed by fire. According to a report by the Freedmen's Bureau, "The city seemed to be under the control of a lawless mob. … All crimes imaginable were committed from simple larceny to rape and murder. Several women and children were shot in bed. One woman (Rachel Johnson) was

A freedmen's school was one of eight schools burned during the Memphis race riot.

shot and then thrown into the flames of a burning house and consumed."

A Louisiana state constitutional convention was held July 30 at the Mechanics Institute in New Orleans. Twenty-six Republican delegates, black and white, met to discuss what the new document should say. They wanted to add an amendment that guaranteed black men the right to vote. The city's mayor and Louisiana's lieutenant governor and attorney general created an all-white police force—composed mainly of veterans of the Confederate army—to disrupt the convention.

As the meeting was beginning, black veterans who had fought for the Union began marching toward the institute from the other side of town. They planned to demonstrate outside the meeting in support of black voting rights. As the soldiers marched down Bourbon Street, they were taunted and pelted with bricks, bottles, and stones. Suddenly shots rang out. L. J. P. Capla, a merchant who had come to watch the convention, later testified: "I saw policemen firing, and shooting the black people; they were shooting poor laboring men, men with their tin buckets in their hands, and even old men walking with sticks. Although they prayed, 'For God's sake, don't shoot us!' they shot them, and when they done that, they tramped upon them, and mashed their heads with their boots, and shot them after they were down." As the veterans, who were outnumbered and outgunned, tried to get into the institute, they were attacked from behind. The police then stormed the building. When the fighting ended, there were nearly 50 people dead and more than 200 wounded.

Members of the Ku Klux Kan wore hoods to disguise their appearance.

As stories like this continued to be reported in the North, more people began siding with former slaves—and Radical Republicans. The president's Reconstruction plan seemed to be a disaster. In the November 1866 congressional elections, voters overwhelmingly cast their ballots for the Republican Party. Suddenly the Republicans had more than a two-thirds majority in Congress. They would be able to pass any legislation they wanted to pass. "The President has no power to control or influence anybody," said Senator James W. Grimes of Iowa, "and legislation will be carried on entirely regardless of his opinions or wishes." The path had been cleared for congressional—radical—reconstruction.

CHAPTER 4
A RADICAL CHANGE

Congress passed the First Reconstruction Act March 2, 1867, over President Johnson's veto. The law divided 10 former Confederate states into military districts and disbanded their governments. (Tennessee, which had ratified the 14th Amendment, had been readmitted to the Union in 1866.) A military governor was to rule each district, and new state elections were to be held. Each state would have to adopt a new state constitution that guaranteed black men the right to vote. Many former Confederates, on the other hand, were denied the right to vote. Congress also passed the Tenure of Office Act—again over Johnson's veto. It prohibited the president from firing any Cabinet members without the consent of the Senate.

Whites in the South were outraged at the idea of allowing black people—former slaves—to vote. They claimed that freedmen were not intelligent enough to cast a ballot. President Johnson gave voice to these concerns in December 1867 when he addressed Congress:

"It is not proposed merely that they shall govern themselves, but that they shall rule the white race, make and administer State laws, elect Presidents and members of Congress, and shape to a greater or less extent the future destiny of the whole country. Would such a trust and power be safe in such hands? ...

"The foundations of society have been broken up by civil war. Industry must be reorganized, justice reestablished, public credit maintained, and order brought out of confusion. To accomplish these ends would require all the wisdom and virtue of the great men who formed our institutions originally. I confidently believe that their descendants will be equal to the

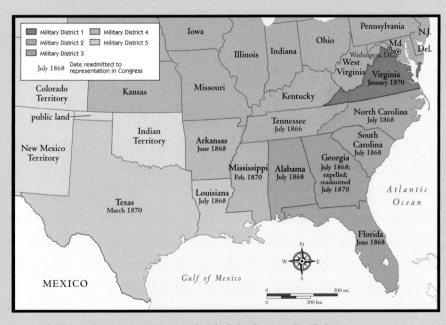

The First Reconstruction Act divided the former Confederacy into five military districts.

arduous [difficult] task before them, but it is worse than madness to expect that Negroes will perform it for us."

The freed people proved detractors like Johnson wrong. Voters took their new right, and responsibility, seriously. Many joined political groups and attended meetings to learn about the issues of the day. "I believe, my friends and fellow citizens, we are not prepared for this suffrage," said Beverly C. Nash, a former slave in South Carolina. "But we can learn. Give a man tools and let him commence to use them, and in time he will learn a trade. So it is with voting. We may not understand it at the start, but in time we shall learn to do our duty."

NAME CALLING

After the war many northerners headed south. Some came to help newly emancipated slaves adjust to freedom. Others came looking for business opportunities. The South needed to be rebuilt. Some northerners re-established plantations and opened factories or mines. Most southern whites resented these invading Yankees, whom they called carpetbaggers after the luggage they carried. They claimed that the carpetbaggers were trying to get rich from the tragedy that had befallen the South. Any southerner who worked with carpetbaggers—or supported the rights of freed blacks—was labeled a scalawag or a traitor.

Hiram Revels was the first African-American member of Congress. He served in the Senate from 1870 to 1871.

Freedmen voted on issues that were important to them and helped bring black people into positions of power for the first time. From local offices such as that of sheriff to the halls of Congress, black people finally had a voice in deciding how they would be governed. During Reconstruction two black men served in the Senate and 14 black men served in the U.S. House. More than 600 were elected to state legislatures.

★A NEW ORDER

In all of the former Confederate states, conventions were held to create new state constitutions. The delegates were a mix of former slaves, freeborn black people, carpetbaggers from the North, and southern white Republicans, known as scalawags. The conventions produced the first public school systems in the South, and some established programs to help the poor. In 1868 Arkansas, Alabama, Florida, Louisiana, North Carolina, and South Carolina were all readmitted to the Union.

THE STANTON DISPUTE

President Lincoln appointed Edwin Stanton secretary of war in 1862. He soon became one of Lincoln's most trusted advisers. Stanton's relationship with Andrew Johnson was not nearly as close. Among other things, Stanton was a fierce supporter of civil rights. Johnson was not. Soon after Congress passed the 1867 Tenure of Office Act, Johnson responded by firing Stanton and giving the position to Ulysses S. Grant. The Senate refused to confirm the action, and Grant voluntarily returned the office to Stanton. In February 1868 Johnson named General Lorenzo Thomas as the new secretary of war. This time Stanton barricaded himself in his office and refused to leave. The dispute was a key factor in Johnson's political undoing.

The restructured southern states were off to a good start, but it was not clear how long the progress would last. A Democratic newspaper in South Carolina angrily offered a prediction: "These constitutions and governments will last just as long as the bayonets which ushered them into being, shall keep them in existence, and not one day longer."

Although President Johnson no longer had the power to stop Congress' Reconstruction plans because of his party's political weakness, he still tried to impede their progress. He began firing the government officials who were trying hardest to enforce the new rules of Reconstruction. But he went a step too far when he fired Secretary of War Edwin Stanton. Citing

Edwin Stanton served as attorney general and secretary of war.

the Tenure of Office Act, the House of Representatives voted to impeach the president. He was saved from being kicked out of office by only one vote in the Senate. Despite all of his problems, Johnson wanted to run for a second term in 1868. Surprising no one, the Democrats chose another candidate, who lost to former Union General Ulysses S. Grant, a Republican.

CHAPTER 5
THE END OF RECONSTRUCTION

When Ulysses S. Grant took the oath of office on March 4, 1869, he promised to deal with the nation's problems "calmly, without prejudice, hate, or sectional pride, remembering that the greatest good to the greatest number is the object to be attained." He was eager to see that Reconstruction be carried out as quickly and as peacefully as possible.

Southerners still had hostile feelings about Reconstruction. Among other things, they charged that the policies were hypocritical. They said northerners were insisting upon rights for southern freedmen that not all black people in the North enjoyed. It was true that when voting rights were established for black males in the South, not all northern states offered the same right. But that wouldn't last long; the 15th Amendment, guaranteeing all black men the right to vote, went into effect in 1870, less than a year after Grant took office.

The desire to spread equality was not the only reason Republicans wanted to give black men the right to vote, however.

Grant won the presidency by only 305,000 votes out of the 5.7 million cast.

Although Grant was a popular war hero, he had not won the presidency with a huge victory margin. Republicans realized that if more black men had been able to vote in New York, Grant would have carried the state instead of losing it to his Democratic opponent, Horatio Seymour. With blacks voting, the Republican Party would have greater support in the entire region.

The 15th Amendment guaranteed that the "right of citizens of the United States to vote shall not be denied or abridged by the United States or by any State on account of race, color, or previous condition of servitude." Black men throughout the country now had the right to vote. After they ratified the amendment, the last of the Confederate states—Georgia, Mississippi, Virginia, and Texas—were allowed to rejoin the Union.

★REDEMPTION REIGNS

What the Constitution said meant nothing to white supremacy groups such as the Ku Klux Klan, and they continued to terrorize blacks throughout the South. They were trying to make African-Americans too scared to exercise their new rights. They also wanted to keep Republicans away from the ballot box. So they terrorized white people who either held office as Republicans or supported the party. These actions aimed to bring the Democratic Party to power in the South and start reversing the progress made by freed people— a process known as Redemption. The followers of the Redemption movement believed that once Democrats

The Ku Klux Klan attacked black families in their homes.

PROMISE UNFULFILLED

Despite the promise of the 15th Amendment, black people in the South did not enjoy the full benefit of the legislation for almost 100 years. Although it was against the law to keep black people from the polls, white southerners after Reconstruction used various methods to do so. Some used literacy tests to deny people the right to vote, some used a poll tax (which poor blacks couldn't afford to pay), and some simply used the very real threat of violence. Most African-Americans in the South were not registered to vote until about 1965. The change came about thanks to the efforts of civil rights workers in the South during the Freedom Summer of 1964 and passage of the Voting Rights Act of 1965.

were in power—and federal troops were removed from the area—the South would be "redeemed." Things would go back to the way they should be—whites on top and blacks with few if any rights.

Local governments were unable—and sometimes unwilling—to stop the violence. In May 1870 Congress passed the first of three Enforcement Acts, which made it a federal offense to attempt to deny anyone his or her civil rights. It had little effect. The second Enforcement

Act, passed in February 1871, established federal supervision over elections. Like the first law, it had little effect on what was happening in the South.

Finally President Grant asked Congress to pass a third act, known as the Ku Klux Klan Act, which it did in April 1871. The law gave the president authority to use federal troops to enforce the 14th and 15th amendments and to make sure people's civil rights were upheld. The act also gave the president the authority to suspend the writ of habeas corpus. That meant authorities could arrest large groups of people without having to bring each suspect to court immediately to be charged.

President Grant (left) signed the Ku Klux Klan Act into law in 1871 at the Capitol.

The U.S. Justice Department in July 1871 told its officials in the South to begin prosecuting Klansmen. Arrests and trials were quickly under way in Mississippi and North Carolina. A firmer hand would need to be taken in South Carolina, however, where Klan activity was particularly bad. On October 12 Grant ordered Klansmen in that state to surrender their weapons and disperse. None complied. Five days later the president suspended habeas corpus in nine South Carolina counties and sent federal troops to help local authorities make arrests. By year's end hundreds of Klansmen had been arrested in South Carolina. In fact, so many arrests were made that the cases almost swamped the court system. Only the worst offenders were prosecuted, while many were released on bail, but the action reduced Klan activity in the area.

★THE BEGINNING OF THE END

The Freedmen's Bureau was disbanded in 1872 because of a lack of funding—and a lack of support from politicians, both Democratic and Republican. Throughout the North, interest in Reconstruction—and civil rights issues—was waning. People seemed to feel that the 13th, 14th, and 15th amendments gave black people enough protections. They also were tired of the conflict. The country was facing an economic crisis. Voters were worried about money and

GOVERNMENT CORRUPTION

President Ulysses S. Grant's presidency might be best remembered for the scandals surrounding his administration. Though Grant was an honest man, he made bad decisions—and ended up surrounding himself with some untrustworthy people.

In 1869 speculators tried to corner the gold market. They were going to buy the nation's gold, causing the price to rise, and then sell their supply at an inflated price. Grant's brother-in-law was in charge of preventing the president from foiling the plan. When Grant got wind of the scheme, he was able to stop the deal, but many people lost money on what came to be called Black Friday.

In 1872 the Crédit Mobilier scandal came to light. A member of the House of Representatives, Oakes Ames of Massachusetts, and another man, Thomas C. Durant, had cheated the government and railroad stockholders out of millions of dollars. It was discovered that several congressmen—and even Grant's vice president, Schuyler Colfax—had accepted bribes to keep quiet.

In 1876 the House of Representatives voted unanimously to impeach William W. Belknap, Grant's secretary of war. He was charged with accepting bribes from corrupt Indian agents. Belknap had resigned shortly before the vote to try to avoid impeachment. He was acquitted by the Senate.

jobs, not how poorly black people were being treated. The lack of interest eroded support for the Republican Party, which was also rocked by several scandals. By 1874 Republican power was declining and Redemption movement governments were gaining power across the South.

The last major piece of Reconstruction legislation to be passed was the Civil Rights Act of 1875. This law guaranteed black people equal treatment in public places. The Supreme Court ruled it unconstitutional in 1883. Many of its provisions didn't become law again until civil rights legislation was passed in the 1960s.

At the time of the presidential election in 1876, only three southern states still had Republican governments. Rutherford B. Hayes, a Civil War hero, was the Republican nominee for president. Samuel Tilden was the Democrats' choice. Thanks in part to the resurgence of the Democratic Party in the South, Tilden won the national popular vote. But Hayes appeared to have won

Rutherford B. Hayes appeared to have won 185 electoral votes to Tilden's 184.

the electoral vote, including the electoral votes of the three southern Republican states. When the Democrats challenged Hayes' electoral victory, citing voting problems in several states, the nation was thrown into a near panic. Americans waited for months to find out who their new president would be. Finally, in March of the following year, the two sides reached what would come to be called the Compromise of 1877. If Hayes promised to remove federal troops from the South, he would be awarded the disputed electoral votes and allowed to take office. Reconstruction was over.

★THE LEGACY OF RECONSTRUCTION

From 1865 to 1877, the United States was the setting of an amazing experiment. Radical Republicans attempted to establish true racial equality in America. The important laws that resulted were designed to protect the civil rights of all citizens. Despite the progress, however, Radical Reconstruction was only a temporary success. It failed when southern whites used violence to "redeem" their states.

The sharecropping system doomed many African-Americans and poor whites to remain in poverty for generations to come. Keeping black people from the polls—through unfair taxes, tests, and intimidation—meant they had little hope for change in their lives. After

An 1874 political cartoon by Thomas Nast charged that the racial abuse suffered by blacks after the Civil War was worse than slavery.

federal troops left the South, African-Americans were quickly stripped of their civil rights. White governments created legislation to replace the Black Codes. These so-called Jim Crow laws once again placed black people in a position inferior to that of whites. (Jim Crow was the name of a character in a popular minstrel show.) In 1883 the Supreme Court ruled that the Civil Rights Act of 1875 was unconstitutional. This decision opened the door to legal segregation, which was made official in the

1896 case *Plessy v. Ferguson.* In it the Supreme Court ruled that separate facilities for blacks and whites were constitutional as long as they were "equal." Though it occurred more often in the South than anywhere else, Jim Crow had become the law of the land.

Under Jim Crow laws, black people were not allowed to share public facilities with whites. That included water fountains, bathrooms, hotels, trains, waiting rooms, and restaurants. Any public facility that was open to both races had a separate section for each. At some restaurants, for example, black people would not be served at the lunch counter. They had to go to the back door and order their food to go. Black and white children also went to separate schools. All of the black schools had inferior equipment and facilities, as well as out-of-date books.

Black people who dared to defy Jim Crow laws faced the threat of physical violence, and the possibility of losing their homes and jobs. They had no hope for legal recourse— everyone in the criminal justice system, from police officers to judges, was white. Lynching was a particularly gruesome method employed by white supremacists to keep black people down. From 1882 to 1968, there were 4,730 known lynchings, including the killings of 3,440 black men and women. These murders were conducted—in public—by mobs throughout the South.

Despite the danger, black people continued to push for

It wasn't until 1954 that the Supreme Court ruled in Brown v. Board of Education *that deliberate public school segregation was illegal.*

equality. During the civil rights movement of the 1950s and 1960s, African-Americans fought for, and finally won, equality before the law. Thanks to the efforts of civil rights workers from across the country, Jim Crow laws were struck down one by one. Without the foundation laid during Reconstruction, especially passage of the 14th and 15th amendments, their struggles—and successes— would have been impossible.

TIMELINE

March: The Freedmen's Bureau is established

April: The Civil War ends; Andrew Johnson becomes president after Abraham Lincoln is assassinated

December: The 13th Amendment, which abolished slavery, is ratified

April: The Civil Rights Act of 1866 is passed over the veto of President Johnson

May: The Ku Klux Klan is created in Tennessee

March: The First and Second Reconstruction Acts are passed; the Third Reconstruction Act is passed in June; the Fourth Reconstruction Act is passed in March 1868

1868

February: The House of Representatives votes to impeach President Johnson; in May the Senate fails by one vote to force Johnson from office

July: The 14th Amendment, which guarantees equal protection, is ratified

1870

February: The 15th Amendment, which grants black men the right to vote, is ratified

May: The first Enforcement Act is passed

1871

February: The second Enforcement Act is passed

April: The Ku Klux Klan Act (also known as the third Enforcement Act) is passed

1872

June: The Freedmen's Bureau is dismantled

1875

March: The Civil Rights Act of 1875 is passed

1877

March: Rutherford B. Hayes becomes president; the last federal troops are withdrawn from the South in April

GLOSSARY

abolitionist: person who supported the immediate end of slavery

amnesty: official pardon or forgiveness for breaking the law

apprentice: someone who learns a trade or craft by working with someone already skilled in the job

Cabinet: group made up of the heads of federal government departments who also advise the president

carpetbagger: derogatory term for a northerner who went to the South after the Civil War either for private gain or to help the South; many of them carried small cloth suitcases called carpetbags

destitute: lacking food, shelter, and clothing

electoral votes: each state has a certain number of electoral votes based on the size of its population; in most states, the candidate who gets the most popular votes in a state wins all of the state's electoral votes

emancipation: the act of freeing a person or a group from bondage

enfranchise: to give the right to vote

expectant: thinking something will happen

hypocritical:	acting in a way that contradicts stated beliefs or feelings
impeach:	to charge an elected official with a serious crime; it can result in removal from office
interracial:	representing or including different races
lenient:	not strict or harsh
oppressor:	someone who treats others in a cruel or unjust manner
quell:	to stop by force
scalawag:	derogatory term for a white southerner who supported Reconstruction governments after the Civil War, either for private gain or to help the South
secede:	withdraw from a nation or group
segregation:	separation of people of different races
suffrage:	the right to vote
supremacy:	possessing the most power
treason:	crime of betraying one's country
vagrancy:	the state of wandering from place to place without a home or job

ADDITIONAL RESOURCES

FURTHER READING

Haskins, James, and Kathleen Benson. *The Rise of Jim Crow.* Tarrytown, N.Y.: Marshall Cavendish Benchmark, 2008.

Haugen, Brenda. *Ulysses S. Grant: Union General and U.S. President.* Minneapolis: Compass Point Books, 2005.

Koestler-Grack, Rachel A. *Abraham Lincoln.* New York: Chelsea House Publishers, 2009.

Osborne, Linda Barrett. *Traveling the Freedom Road: From Slavery and the Civil War Through Reconstruction.* New York: Abrams Books for Young Readers, 2009.

Perritano, John. *Radical Republicans.* New York: Crabtree Publishing Co., 2009.

Raatma, Lucia. *The Carpetbaggers.* Minneapolis: Compass Point Books, 2005.

Ruggiro, Adriane. *American Voices from Reconstruction.* New York: Marshall Cavendish Benchmark, 2007.

INTERNET SITES

FactHound offers a safe, fun way to find Internet sites related to this book. All of the sites on FactHound have been researched by our staff.

Here's all you do:

Visit *www.facthound.com*

Type in this code: 9780756543709

Read all the books in the Civil War series:

A Nation Divided: The Long Road to the Civil War

Bull Run to Gettysburg: Early Battles of the Civil War

North Over South: Final Victory in the Civil War

Reconstruction: Rebuilding America after the Civil War

SELECT BIBLIOGRAPHY

Abraham Lincoln Online. http://showcase.netins.net/web/creative/lincoln/speeches/last.htm

Africana Archives: Freedmen's Bureau Records at The University of South Florida Africana Heritage Project. www.africanaheritage.com/Freedmens_Bureau.asp

America's Reconstruction: People and Politics After the Civil War. www.digitalhistory.uh.edu/reconstruction/introduction.html

The Avalon Project: Documents in Law, History and Diplomacy. http://avalon.law.yale.edu/subject_menus/19th.asp

Budiansky, Stephen. *The Bloody Shirt: Terror After Appomattox*. New York: Viking, 2008.

Conlin, Joseph R. *The American Past: A Survey of American History*. Boston: Wadsworth/Cengage Learning, 2009.

Du Bois, W.E.B. *Black Reconstruction in America 1860–1880*. New York: The Free Press, 1998.

Dudley, William, ed. *Reconstruction*. San Diego: Greenhaven Press, 2003.

Dunning, Richard Archibald. *Reconstruction Political and Economic, 1865–1877*. New York: Harper and Brothers, 1907.

Foner, Eric. *Reconstruction: America's Unfinished Revolution, 1863–1877*. New York: Harper & Row, 1988.

Foster, Lillian. *Andrew Johnson, President of the United States; His Life and Speeches*. New York: Richardson and Co., 1866.

Grant Administration Scandals. www.u-s-history.com/pages/h234.html

The History Cooperative. www.historycooperative.org/journals/jala/1/neely.html

Hollandsworth, James G., Jr. *An Absolute Massacre: The New Orleans Race Riot of July 30, 1866*. Baton Rouge: Louisiana State University Press, 2001.

Hyslop, Stephen G. *Eyewitness to the Civil War: The Complete History from Secession to Reconstruction*. Washington, D.C.: National Geographic Society, 2006.

McKenzie, Robert Tracy. *One South or Many? Plantation Belt and Upcountry in Civil War-Era Tennessee*. New York: Cambridge University Press, 1994.

McPherson, James. *Battle Cry of Freedom: The Civil War Era*. New York: Oxford University Press, 2003.

The National Archives: African American Records. www.archives.gov/research/african-americans/#at

Patrick, Rembert W. *The Reconstruction of the Nation*. New York: Oxford University Press, 1967.

The People's Vote: 100 Documents That Shaped America. www.usnews.com/usnews/documents/docpages/document_page37.htm

Primary Documents in American History. Library of Congress. www.loc.gov/rr/program/bib/ourdocs/15thamendment.html

Reconstruction: The Second Civil War. www.pbs.org/wgbh/amex/reconstruction

South Carolina Ku Klux Klan Trials: 1871–72 The Ku Klux Klan Act. http://law.jrank.org/pages/2612/South-Carolina-Ku-Klux-Klan-Trials-1871-72-Ku-Klux-Klan-Act.html

Sterling, Dorothy, ed. *The Trouble They Seen: The Story of Reconstruction in the Words of African Americans*. New York: Da Capo Press, 1994.

Walker, David, and Henry Highland Garnet. *Walker's Appeal in Four Articles: An Address to the Slaves of the United States of America*. New York: Cosimo Classics, 2005.

SOURCE NOTES

Page 4, line 11: Abraham Lincoln's Last Public Address. 11 April 1865. 5 March 2010. http://showcase.netins.net/web/creative/lincoln/speeches/last.htm

Page 6, line 10: James McPherson. *Battle Cry of Freedom: The Civil War Era.* New York: Oxford University Press, 2003, p. 854.

Page 7, sidebar, line 9: The Emancipation Proclamation. National Archives and Records Administration. 5 March 2010. www.archives.gov/exhibits/featured_documents/emancipation_proclamation/transcript.html

Page 9, line 11: Lincoln Reconstruction Plan. 5 March 2010. www.u-s-history.com/pages/h177.html

Page 11, sidebar, line 8: Meeting Between Black Religious Leaders and Union Military Authorities, 12 Jan. 1865. Freedmen & Southern Society Project. 5 March 2010. www.history.umd.edu/Freedmen/savmtg.htm

Page 11, sidebar, line 21: Forty Acres and a Mule: Special Field Order No. 15 by William Tecumseh Sherman. 16 Jan. 1865. 5 March 2010. http://teachingamericanhistory.org/library/index.asp?document=545

Page 13, line 7: *American Experience Reconstruction: The Second Civil War.* 5 March 2010. www.pbs.org/wgbh/amex/reconstruction/players/vb_schools_tr_qt.html

Page 14, sidebar, line 10: David Walker and Henry Highland Garnet. *Walker's Appeal in Four Articles: An Address to the Slaves of the United States of America.* New York: Cosimo Classics, 2005, p. 37.

Page 14, sidebar, line 14: David Walker. 5 March 2010. www.africawithin.com/bios/david_walker.htm

Page 15, line 5: America's Reconstruction: People and Politics After the Civil War. 5 March 2010. www.digitalhistory.uh.edu/reconstruction/section2/section2_school.html

Page 16, line 4: Dorothy Sterling, ed. *The Trouble They Seen: The Story of Reconstruction in the Words of African Americans.* New York: Da Capo Press, 1994, p. 21.

Page 19, sidebar, line 17: Thaddeus Stevens Biography. Thaddeus Stevens College of Technology. 5 March 2010. www.stevenscollege.edu/301396.ihtml

Page 20, line 17: Reconstruction. Digital History. 5 March 2010. www.digitalhistory.uh.edu/historyonline/us21.cfm

Page 21, line 16: Should Andrew Johnson Be Impeached? Digital History. 5 March 2010. www.digitalhistory.uh.edu/historyonline/con_johnson.cfm

Page 22, line 22: Ibid.

Page 23, line 5: Joseph R. Conlin. *The American Past: A Survey of American History.* Boston: Wadsworth Cengage Learning, 2010, p. 402.

Page 23, line 13: Stephen Budiansky. T*he Bloody Shirt: Terror After Appomattox.* New York: Viking, 2008, p. 22.

Page 24, sidebar, line 4: 13th Amendment to the U.S. Constitution: Abolition of Slavery (1865). 5 March 2010. www.ourdocuments.gov/doc.php?flash=old&doc=40

Page 29, line 8: The Southern "Black Codes" of 1865–66. Constitutional Rights Foundation. 5 March 2010. www.crf-usa.org/bill-of-rights-in-action/bria-15-2-c.html

Page 29, line 13: Mark E. Neely Jr. *The Lincoln Theme Since Randall's Call: The Promises and Perils of Professionalism.* Papers of the Abraham Lincoln Association. 5 March 2010. www.historycooperative.org/journals/jala/1/neely.html

Page 29, line 17: William Archibald Dunning. *Reconstruction, Political and Economic, 1865–1877.* New York: Harper and Brothers, 1907, p. 57.

Page 30, line 10: From Revolution to Reconstruction: Documents: Thaddeus Stevens Speech of December 18, 1865. 5 March 2010. www.let.rug.nl/usa/D/1851-1875/reconstruction/steven.htm

Page 31, sidebar, line 6: Howard Means. *The Avenger Takes His Place: Andrew Johnson and the 45 Days That Changed the Nation.* Orlando: Harcourt Inc., p. 176.

Page 31, line 7: *American Experience Reconstruction: The Second Civil War.*

Page 32, line 1: Lillian Foster. *Andrew Johnson, His Life and Speeches.* New York: Richardson & Co., 1866. Veto of the Civil Rights Bill by Andrew Johnson. 5 March 2010. http://teachingamericanhistory.org/library/index.asp?document=1944

Page 32, line 9: Edward Belcher Callender. *Thaddeus Stevens: Commoner.* Boston: A. Williams and Company, 1882, p. 140.

Page 32, line 16: U.S. Constitution: Fourteenth Amendment. FindLaw. 5 March 2010. http://caselaw.lp.findlaw.com/data/constitution/amendment14/

Page 34, line 14: Robert Tracy McKenzie. *One South or Many? Plantation Belt and Upcountry in Civil War-Era Tennessee.* New York.: Cambridge University Press, 1994, p. 127.

Page 35, line 5: Memphis Race Riot of 1866. Tennessee Encyclopedia of Race and Culture. 5 March 2010. http://tennesseeencyclopedia.net/imagegallery.php?EntryID=M080

Page 35, line 9: Memphis History: The Race Riots of 1866. 5 March 2010. www.memphishistory.org/Events/TheRaceRiotsof1866/Page3/tabid/383/Default.aspx

Page 36, line 19: *Report of the Select Committee on the New Orleans Riots by the House Committee on the New Orleans Riots, 1866–1867*, p. 120. 5 March 2010. ww.archive.org/stream/reportofselectco03unit#page/120/mode/2up

Page 37, line 6: James G. Hollandsworth Jr. *An Absolute Massacre: The New Orleans Race Riot of July 30, 1866.* Baton Rouge: Louisiana State University Press, 2001, p. 3.

Page 37, line 22: Eric Foner. *Reconstruction, 1863–1877: America's Unfinished Revolution.* New York: Harper & Rowe 1988, p. 271

Page 39, line 1: Andrew Johnson: Third Annual Message, 3 Dec. 1867. The American Presidency Project. 5 March 2010. www.presidency.ucsb.edu/ws/index.php?pid=29508

Page 40, line 6: W.E.B. Du Bois. *Black Reconstruction in America 1860–1880.* New York: The Free Press, 1998, p. 391.

Page 41, line 6: Stephen G. Hyslop. *Eyewitness to the Civil War: The Complete History from Secession to Reconstruction.* Washington, D.C.: National Geographic Society, 2006, p. 390.

Page 41, line 7: Reconstruction, 1863–1877: America's Unfinished Revolution, p. 355.

Page 43, line 4: Ibid., p. 333.

Page 44, line 2: First Inaugural Address of Ulysses S. Grant. 4 March 1869. 5 March 2010. http://avalon.law.yale.edu/19th_century/grant1.asp

Page 45, line 20: A Century of Lawmaking for a New Nation: U.S. Congressional Documents and Debates, 1774–1875. 5 March 2010. http://memory.loc.gov/cgi-bin/ampage?collId=llsl&fileName=015/llsl015.db&recNum=379

Page 54, line 22: Jim Crow Museum, Ferris State University. 5 March 2010. www.ferris.edu/JIMCROW/what.htm

INDEX

ABOUT THE AUTHOR

Stephanie Fitzgerald has been writing nonfiction for young people for more than 10 years, and she is the author of more than 20 books. Her specialties include history, wildlife, and popular culture. Stephanie lives in Stamford, Connecticut, with her husband and their daughter.